George M. Towle

England in Egypt

George M. Towle

England in Egypt

ISBN/EAN: 9783337239909

Printed in Europe, USA, Canada, Australia, Japan

Cover: Foto ©ninafisch / pixelio.de

More available books at **www.hansebooks.com**

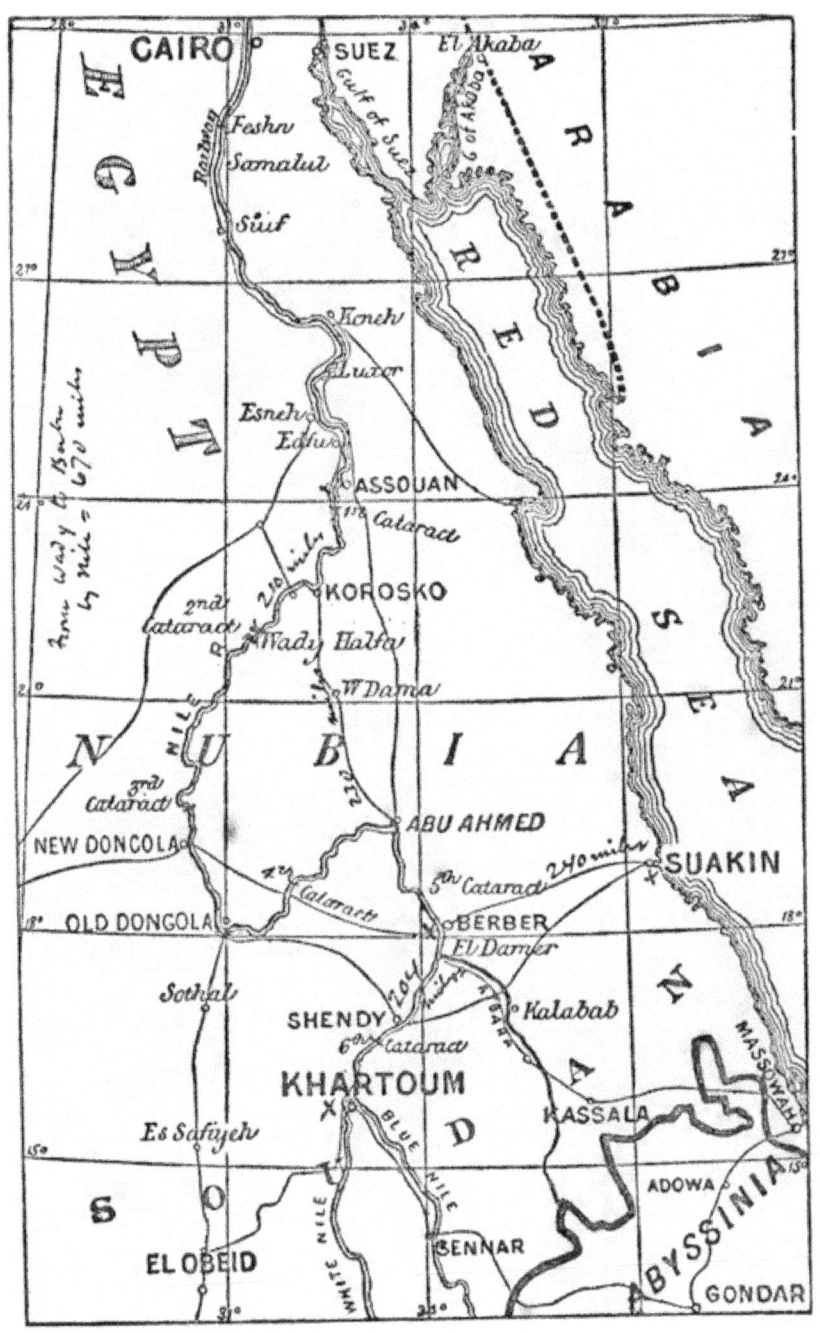

VALLEY OF THE NILE.

TIMELY TOPICS

ENGLAND IN EGYPT

BY

GEORGE MAKEPEACE TOWLE

AUTHOR OF "ENGLAND AND RUSSIA IN ASIA," "MODERN GREECE," ETC.

With Maps

BOSTON
TICKNOR AND COMPANY
1886

Copyright, 1885

By TICKNOR AND COMPANY.

All rights reserved

PRESS OF
ROCKWELL AND CHURCHILL
BOSTON

PREFACE.

THE interference of England in the affairs of Egypt, and the results which have flowed therefrom, have for several years attracted the world's attention by a succession of striking and often thrilling and dramatic events. To those who study those events, even superficially, a distinct connection will appear between the establishment by England of a dominant influence in Egypt, and the attitude of England towards Russia in the East. Both are parts of the historic and constantly recurring Eastern Question. Had not Russian aggression in the East threatened Constantinople and India, it is scarcely conceivable that England would ever have deeply concerned herself in the affairs of Egypt.

This volume aims to present in a clear light

the history of Egypt during the last seventy years; the present internal condition of the country; the conquest and character of the region of the Soudan; the rise of the "False Prophet;" the reasons for which and the processes by which English influence in Egypt has been acquired; and the events, both in Egypt and in the Soudan, which have taken place as a consequence of English interference.

G. M. T.

BOSTON, October, 1885.

CONTENTS.

		PAGE
I.	Modern Egypt	9
II.	The Suez Canal	30
III.	The Government, People and Resources of Egypt	41
IV.	The Soudan	55
V.	El Mahdi, the "False Prophet"	62
VI.	England in Egypt and the Soudan	74

LIST OF MAPS.

VALLEY OF THE NILE . . . . *Frontispiece*

FORTRESS OF THE SOUDAN . *facing page* 58

KHARTOUM AND ENVIRONS . " " 84

ENGLAND IN EGYPT.

I.

MODERN EGYPT.

THE history of modern Egypt began with the foundation of the semi-feudal dynasty of the present reigning house by Mehemet Ali, in 1811. For three centuries Egypt had been under the rule of the Sultans of Turkey, and had received its governors from Constantinople. Yet even before the rise of Mehemet Ali, the authority of the Sultans in the land of the Nile had not been absolute. It had always been more or less modified by the great Egyptian military caste, which while conceding the feudal dependence of Egypt on

Turkey, maintained the government of the Mamlouk chiefs. The virtual ruler of Egypt was a native Bey, chosen by Beys. It was he who levied taxes, kept up a military force, coined money, and performed other acts of local sovereignty. The principal visible sign of Turkish ascendency appeared in the annual tribute which was paid by Egypt into the coffers of the Sultan.

Revolts to throw off the Turkish yoke altogether had taken place before that which, under Mehemet Ali, conferred upon Egypt a virtual though not as yet an acknowledged independence. These former revolts had not prevailed; but the hold of the Sultans had always been too weak to enable them to punish or degrade the revolting Beys. The invasion of Egypt by Napoleon well-nigh destroyed all semblance of Turkish authority on the Nile, which was only restored by the subsequent naval triumphs of England; always, for her own reasons, the prop and protector of the Turk. Yet even after Nelson had turned the tide of war in the Mediterranean at Trafalgar, the Beys were strong enough to depose, and even on one occasion to execute, the viceroys sent by the Sultan to rule over his uncomfortable dependency.

Mehemet Ali, who in the history of Eastern politics holds a rank of the first magnitude as a warrior and a statesman, and to whose genius Egypt owes at least a far higher position among the nations than ever since the time of her ancient splendor and power, was by birth a Macedonian, and by profession a soldier in the armies of the Sultan. He was as much a foreigner in Egypt as any Turkish viceroy. At the age of thirty-seven he had already won high military rank by reason of his extraordinary capacity, and found himself holding an important command in Egypt. Although he had fought vigorously against the disloyal Beys, he contrived to win the respect and even the affection of the Egyptians. Suddenly he was proclaimed viceroy by the native chiefs at Cairo; and so feeble at this time was the Sultan's grasp on Egypt, that he actually withdrew his own viceroy, and acknowledged Mehemet Ali in his stead.

No sooner had Mehemet Ali found himself in power than he set about building up a strong nationality. He suppressed the military aristocracy of the Mamlouks, which struggled against his promotion; he reorganized the Egyptian forces; he conquered Syria; and he compelled Turkey to acknowledge by treaty his sovereignty, subject to feudal tribute, over Egypt and its recent acquisitions. So aggressive indeed became Mehemet Ali's military aspirations, that he is believed to have cherished an ambition to conquer European Turkey itself. In a brief war with the Sultan, Mehemet's son, Ibrahim Pasha, completely defeated the Turkish forces. Europe, alarmed lest Constantinople itself should be attacked, intervened in the humiliated Sultan's favor. An English fleet proceeded to the Eastern waters; Mehemet Ali's victorious progress was checked, and Syria was restored to the Sultan.

But Mehemet Ali gained one important advantage from this international interference. By a treaty, of which the signatories were

Turkey, England, Russia and Austria, concluded in 1840, his right to Egyptian sovereignty was acknowledged, and this was declared hereditary in his family. The principal restrictions imposed by this treaty on the viceroy were, that he should pay a large annual tribute to the Porte; that his army should not be increased beyond a certain stated limit; and that he should hold no direct diplomatic relations with other powers. Mehemet Ali was wise and shrewd enough to accept this settlement in good faith. He had won the sanction of the great powers to his viceregal powers; he had shown the Sultan that his military prowess was not to be despised; and he had long subdued all serious opposition to his rule among the Egyptians themselves.

He now directed his great abilities exclusively to the reorganization of Egypt as a State, and here his remarkable administrative genius found abundant scope. The system of Egyptian government which exists to-day was in the main Mehemet Ali's creation and handiwork; and, debased as

Egypt is beneath the autocratic control of the foreigner, there are many traces through its present administrative constitution of a master-hand in State craft. It is declared, on high authority, to be "incomparably the most civilized and efficient of existing Mussulman governments." Many abuses of centuries' growth and standing were abolished; order was imparted to the official services; education was somewhat promoted; the finances were placed on a sounder basis, and the industries of Egypt were diligently fostered by this able sovereign.

Mehemet Ali died in his eightieth year, in 1848. His successors for the most part continued his policy of internal reform and constructive energy. He was succeeded by his warlike son Ibrahim, whose reign, however, only lasted four months. Ibrahim was succeeded by his nephew, Abbas, the least worthy of Mehemet's successors. Abbas was weak, dissolute and unambitious, and fortunately his rule was also brief. He died in 1854, giving place to Said Pasha, Mehemet

Ali's third son. At this time the order of succession to the Egyptian throne, like that in Turkey, was that the eldest male of the reigning family, and not necessarily the eldest son, succeeded. Said Pasha was altogether superior to Abbas. He did much to repair the injuries in the State which the weakness and selfishness of Abbas had inflicted. But Said was wanting in the vigorous will of his father; and during the nine years of his reign Egypt made but slow progress in civil and political development.

Said's successor was Ismail Pasha, son of the viceroy Ibrahim, and grandson of Mehemet Ali. Ismail reigned from 1863 to 1879. It was during the sixteen years of his rule that the circumstances arose which brought foreign interference upon Egypt. Ismail was a singular combination of energy, extravagance, cruelty and self-indulgence. In many ways he certainly advanced the material interests of Egypt; but the general result of his rule was to plunge Egypt into an indebtedness which formed the pretext for foreign interference, and to reduce his dynasty to vassalage to England. Ismail was a man of European education and experience. He had studied long in Paris, and when as a young man he returned from France to Egypt, he was probably the most cultivated person in the kingdom. Under his uncle Said he filled some of the highest offices of the State, and conducted a campaign in the Soudan with success and honor.

No sooner had he become viceroy than his executive ability and vigor became apparent. The result of the exercise of these qualities soon appeared in the prosecution and completion of great public works, the expansion of the Egyptian revenues, and the revival of Egyptian commerce. He seemed determined to confer upon his country all the material benefits of European civilization. Canals, railways, docks, harbors and telegraphs were created with magical rapidity. The viceroy personally directed these improvements, and was noted for the assiduity with which he devoted himself to his official labors. He was, moreover, one of the most suave and accessible of men. Yet his rule was in many respects harsh, despotic, and cruel. He ground down his people with oppressive taxes, and amassed for himself a colossal fortune from their toil. The leading features of his reign may be briefly reviewed.

In 1866, by means of a heavy bribe, Ismail persuaded the Sultan to grant him the title of Khidiv-el-Misr (King of Egypt); which caused the Egyptian sovereign to be usually called "the Khedive." But the Sultan's concessions did not end with the royal title. He also changed the order of Egyptian succession, which he ordained should descend no longer to the nearest male relative, but to the eldest son of the last Khedive. Thus the Egyptian law of succession was conformed to that of the European powers. In return for these concessions the annual tribute from Egypt to the Sultan was raised from $1,880,000 to $3,600,000. Another bribe, offered and accepted nine years later, induced the Sultan to grant the Khedive the right, hitherto forbidden, to send envoys to foreign courts, and to maintain an independent Egyptian army. Thus the ties between Egypt and Turkey were considerably loosened, and the Khedive began to feel himself to be a true sovereign.

The finances of Egypt, under Ismail's extravagant rule, became more and more involved, as he himself became richer, and as the vast public works which he undertook proceeded to completion. By a habit of almost constant and reckless borrowing Ismail piled the debt of Egypt to stupendous figures. When he came to the Khedivate that debt amounted to only about $16,000,000. In the last year of his reign it was not far from $400,000,000. It is not easy to say how much the debt is now (1885); but it certainly exceeds the latter figures. This indebtedness, it need scarcely be said, mainly took the form of bonds, which were placed on the European markets. The loans thus created, therefore, established the creditors of Egypt in almost every European country, but principally in England and in France. Of course in each case that a loan was made, Egypt was compelled to pay a higher interest, and to accept less than the nominal amount of the loan.

A few examples of these loans may make the desperate financial situation at which Egypt arrived under Ismail more clear. The connection of Egypt with the Suez canal, and the financial complications arising therefrom, must be reserved for a separate chapter on that great work. In Ismail's first year he effected a loan of $28,000,000, at 7 per cent.; but he only received $24,400,000. Two years later he effected a loan for $15,000,000, to complete the Alexandria and Suez railway, at 8 per cent., receiving however only $13,000,000. In 1868 he effected a loan of $59,500,000, which cost him a yearly interest of $13\frac{1}{4}$ per cent., and yielded him in actual cash only $36,000,000. This loan was intended to relieve the congested floating debt, and to finish certain public works under way. By 1873, ten years after Ismail's succession, the unfunded liabilities of Egypt had reached the sum of $130,000,000, for which Egypt had to pay an average annual interest of no less than 14 per cent.

Five of Ismail's extravagant loans, which nominally footed up $279,000,000, had only brought him, in actual cash, $175,000,000; but he had to pay interest on the larger sum. Nor were these public debts the only debts contracted by this magnificently lavish prince. He had also hypothecated his private estates, which are known in Egypt as the " daïra," to the lips. These estates comprised over 400,000 acres of arable land, besides a large number of sugar and other factories. Ismail erected factories on his estates during his reign which cost at least $30,000,000. With the properties of his estates and his civil list, which was also at his personal disposal, his income was something like $2,550,000. A succession of loans on the " daïra " loaded it, as the national treasury had been loaded, with a debt of $45,000,000.

In 1875 the finances of Egypt were temporarily relieved by the sale of the Khedive's shares in the Suez canal to the British government. By this dramatic operation of Lord Beaconsfield, then Premier, the Egyptian treasury received the sum of $19,882,915. The crisis of insolvency was delayed, not averted. The time had now arrived for the beginning of European intervention in the affairs of Egypt. The creditors of Egypt became alarmed, then clamorous. It may be that the two powers chiefly interested in Egyptian finances — England and France — saw a political as well as a financial advantage in the necessity for securing the interest on the loans to their subjects who were Egyptian creditors. At all events, the payment of that interest had become a grave subject of inquiry and of doubt; and whether the interference was merely a pretext for subsequent political control, or whether it was a *bona-fide* attempt to secure Egypt's creditors, it was entered upon, and has steadily continued to the present day.

The first step in the direction of foreign interference was taken by Ismail himself. Egypt was on the verge of brankruptcy, and he felt compelled to call in outside assistance. Accordingly he asked the British government to send two financial experts to Cairo, to examine into and effect a reform in the financial system of his kingdom. The result was, that Mr. Stephen Cave, M.P., arrived at Cairo late in 1875. His instructions were to investigate Egyptian finances and report thereon to the English authorities. Mr. Cave spent two months on his task, and then submitted his report. He declared that the Egyptian treasury was solvent, and made certain recommendations, which need not be here described, by which its bankruptcy might be averted.

Mr. Cave, however, was an investigating agent only, and was not armed with diplomatic powers. So in the summer of 1876, Mr. George J. Goschen, M.P., was sent to Cairo, to negotiate with the Khedive some method by which the financial difficulty might be solved. The French creditors of Egypt had now become actively interested in the subject, and had already proposed an abortive scheme to the Khedive. It was deemed best by England and France that they should coöperate in bringing about a reform in Egyptian finance. To Mr. Goschen, therefore, was joined M. Joubert, as representing French interests. These joint envoys finally agreed upon a scheme completely reorganizing the conditions of the Egyptian debt, considerably reducing its sum total, its rate of redemption, and the amounts of interest to be paid. To this scheme the Khedive reluctantly assented; and it became the law of Egypt by his decree.

The inevitable result of the adoption of the Goschen-Joubert scheme was the establishment of a joint English and French financial control in Egypt. It became necessary that the powers should secure some stronger guarantee than the Khedive's consent that the scheme would be carried out in good faith. What has since been called the "dual control" speedily followed. A joint English and French administration of finance was established in 1877 at Cairo. At its head were two "Controllers-General," one English and one French. To one of these was assigned the power and duty to collect the revenues of Egypt, and to distribute the collected revenue among the several departments. The other had charge of the audit of the treasury, and of the public debt. Both were invested with well-nigh absolute authority in these functions. The Controller-General of Receipts exercised full powers over the tax collectors. No tax could be levied without the approval of his signature. The Controller-General of Audit had full power over the treasury accounts and those of the public offices. No departmental checks or orders for payment were valid unless countersigned by him.

The appointment of the Controllers-General was for a period of five years. They were directly responsible to the Khedive. They were a committee, acting in coöperation with the finance minister, to decide upon all the larger governmental contracts. They were supplied with ample subsidiary machinery for carrying out their task. Two sub-commissions, one of the public debt, and the other of the railways and the port of Alexandria, were included in the scheme. The first of these sub-commissions was composed entirely of Englishmen and Frenchmen, and was intrusted with receiving and paying into the Bank of England the revenue for paying the debt annuities. The second of the sub-commissions comprised two Egyptian, one French, and two English members, and had in charge the receiving and paying over of the revenues derived from the railways and the Alexandria port receipts. The dual control, thus set up at Cairo, in spite of all the guarantees and safeguards by which it was hedged about, was short-lived. It had not been in operation two years before it became evident that Ismail Pasha himself was tired of the arrangement, and restive under the restrictions of foreign surveillance. Egyptian statesmen, and certain sections of the Egyptian people, became hostile to the interference imposed by the powers. Financial control necessarily involved, to a greater or less extent, control over the political affairs of the Khedivate also. A growing feeling of jealousy grew up throughout the native administration. Something like a patriotic party was formed.

It is declared by some that this unfriendly sentiment towards the control was manufactured by Ismail himself, in order to afford him an excuse for retreating from his engagements. Others say that he was forced by the threat of revolution to take the course he did. It is likely enough that each of these opinions is a half truth. Ismail did not discourage the growth of a patriotic party, and was probably glad that its rise should afford him a pretext to relieve himself of the restraints of the foreigner. At all events, in the spring of 1879 he issued a decree abolishing the control, and resuming the native management of the finances. Nubar Pasha, his premier, a Christian and a friend of the Anglo-French policy, resigned office and left Egypt.

But now Ismail found himself face to face with the great powers of Europe. Prince Bismarck, speaking with the might of Germany at his back, protested against the Khedive's course, and instigated the Sultan, still nominally the master of Egypt, to bring pressure upon the Khedive. The next event was the sudden deposition and banishment of Ismail Pasha. This was brought about, with the approval and coöperation of Bismarck, by the influence of England and France. In his place his eldest son, Tewfik Pasha, was installed as Khedive of Egypt; and, from that day to this, Tewfik has remained unresistingly under the control of England. The dual control was restored, with enlarged powers. The supervision of the Controllers-General now extended beyond the region of finance into that of the general political condition of the kingdom. This restored and enlarged control was established by a decree of Tewfik in November, 1879.

The fresh arrangement lasted, with more or less friction, about two years and a half. The new Khedive proved to be weak, vacillating, timorous, easily swayed and cravenly submissive to his European masters. No doubt the financial and material condition of Egypt was somewhat improved. On the other hand, the Egyptians felt more and more keenly the pressure and the humiliation of foreign interference. As time advanced, the symptoms of grave discontent became more apparent. The army was now honeycombed with disaffection. Its officers were almost to a man hostile to the control, and Tewfik was despised and detested by the overwhelming majority of his subjects.

In the summer of 1882 the revolt in the army against the control grew ripe. At the head of the rebellious soldiery was Arabi Pasha, the Minister of War. Arabi was an able soldier, a statesman of proved ability, and a patriot whose sincerity it is difficult to doubt. At last he put himself at the front of the national cause. He virtually made Tewfik a prisoner in his palace, and took possession of Alexandria with the troops. England now took prompt action. She proposed to France a joint expedition to put down the military insurrection. France refused, withdrew from further active interference in Egyptian affairs, and thenceforth continued isolated therefrom. England assumed the task alone, and thus acquired the sole responsibility of control in Egypt which she has ever since retained.

The British war fleet was sent to Alexandria;

and that ancient city was bombarded, almost destroyed, and taken from the insurgents. A fire broke out, which completed the destruction begun by the bombs of the "Invincible" and the "Inflexible." Arabi retreated in good order. But the English were prompt in his pursuit. A well-appointed army under Sir Garnet Wolseley encountered the rebel force at Tel-el-Kebir, not far from Cairo, completely defeated Arabi, destroyed the flower of the Egyptian army, and returned in triumph with Arabi as prisoner. Arabi was tried for high treason and condemned to death. But the English government interposed, and the rebel chief's sentence was commuted to exile for life. He was sent to Ceylon, where he is still virtually an English prisoner. From the time of the battle of Tel-el-Kebir England became practically the sole mistress of Egypt; and the account of the later events under her rule will be given in a subsequent chapter.

II.

THE SUEZ CANAL.

THE successful construction of the Suez canal materially modified the politics of Europe, changed both the internal and the external status of Egypt, and gave a new channel of transit to the commerce between Europe and Asia. It substituted for the long water way around the Cape of Good Hope one which reduced the time of transit between Europe and Asia by about one-half. That such a communication should be actually established was a matter of very grave political moment to several of the European powers. It lessened the military as well as the commercial route to India, and this was a matter of high importance to England. The same fact caused Russia to look with jealous eye upon its completion. Having been constructed, moreover, by a French company, and to a large extent by French capital, it was an enterprise in which France had an immediate concern.

The project of M. Ferdinand de Lesseps to pierce the Isthmus of Suez with a canal, thus joining the waters of the Mediterranean to those of the Red Sea, was by no means the first which had been conceived with that end in view. Far back in the time of the Pharaohs (about 1400 B.C.) a canal fifty-seven miles long is said to have been built on the isthmus. Darius made a similar attempt to unite the two seas, and it seems to be proved that a complete canal actually existed and was used some three centuries before Christ. The first Napoleon caused a survey of the isthmus to be made while he was in possession of Egypt; and later Mehemet Ali seriously contemplated the construction of a canal. But all these projects proved abortive until M. de Lesseps had matured the scheme which, amid many formidable obstacles and much ridicule, he at last carried to successful completion.

Ferdinand de Lesseps, when quite a young

man, was a clerk in the French consulate at Cairo. As far back as 1830 he had begun to brood over the idea that a canal might be made, and to picture to himself the vast influence which such a canal could not fail to have on the relations and destiny of nations. This dream occupied his mind and his studies for a quarter of a century. It was not until 1854, however, that Lesseps had matured his plan, and was ready to broach it to the Egyptian ruler. Said Pasha was then reigning, and from the first looked with a certain degree of favor on Lesseps's project. He gave him a preliminary concession for a canal across the isthmus, and two years later made this concession a final one. Lesseps, knowing how deeply interested England must be in such a water way if completed, applied to Lord Palmerston, then Prime Minister, for pecuniary aid in prosecuting the scheme. Palmerston only laughed him to scorn, declared the project impossible, and vigorously opposed Lesseps's operations.

The enthusiastic engineer was not to be dismayed by such a rebuff. Turning to his own country, Lesseps received prompt and substantial encouragement. A company to construct the canal was formed with a capital of $40,000,000, in shares of $100, more than half of which was speedily taken up, for the most part in France. In 1860 Said Pasha, convinced that the canal would be a great thing for Egypt, assumed all the shares yet unsold, which amounted to $17,500,000. Turkey, as the suzerain of Egypt, forbade the undertaking; but it is a striking evidence how feeble Turkish power had become in the land of the Nile, that no attention was paid to the Sultan's prohibition, and that M. Lesseps pursued his undertaking just as if no such potentate as the Sultan existed.

Ground was broken on the Suez canal on the 25th of April, 1859, near the site where the busy town of Port Said (named in honor of Said Pasha) has since grown up. A large part of the workmen were Egyptian fellahs, who had been subject to a forced conscription, called the *corvée*, and were paid cheap wages by the company. Owing to the interference of the English government this supply of native workmen was withdrawn just as the canal was getting fairly under way. The English also persuaded Ismail that the company, under the concessions made to it, would be too powerful from a political point of view. The issue of the differences which thus arose between the company and the Egyptian government was, that all matters of disagreement were referred to the Emperor Napoleon III.

The Emperor awarded the company an indemnity of $17,500,000, to be paid by Egypt for the loss of the *corvée*, for the withdrawal of certain concessions of land, and for the resumption of the fresh-water canal. This added capital enabled the company to steadily pursue its great project. In 1864, however, Lesseps was obliged to negotiate a loan founded on lottery drawings, to the amount of $33,330,000. A still further loan was contracted five years later of $6,000,000, and Egypt paid the company $6,000,000 more for the giving up of all rights on the fresh-water canal. The total capital of the company had now grown to $85,000,000; and this sum increased later to $95,000,000. The construction of the canal occupied a little more than ten years; and its completion was celebrated in November, 1869, by imposing *fêtes* and ceremonies, at which the Empress of the French and many European notabilities assisted.

The Suez canal, in its complete course, from the Mediterranean to the Gulf of Suez, is 86 miles long. Its width at the water line varies from 190 feet to 328 feet. Its width at the bottom averages 72 feet. Its depth is 26 feet. It is supplied with numerous "sidings," by which large vessels can be shunted so as to allow others to pass in the narrower parts of the channel. At its opening the canal was available for vessels drawing 18 feet, but the widenings since made have considerably increased this capacity. Up to within a recent period the canal has proved sufficient for the requirements of commercial transit; but latterly it has become overcrowded, and several schemes — one for still further widening it, and another for constructing a new canal parallel to it — have been gravely considered and debated.

It is important, from both a political and a commercial point of view, to show how the Suez canal has shortened the water way from the great emporiums of Europe and America to those of the Orient. In his valuable book on Egypt, Mr. J. C. McCoan gives the following statement as to the saving of time and distance effected by the canal as compared with the route around the Cape of Good Hope: "By the latter (the cape) the distance between England and Bombay is 10,860 nautical miles, while by the canal it is only 6,020 miles, representing a saving of 4,840 miles; from Marseilles to Bombay the distance by the cape is 10,560 miles, by the canal 4,620 miles, or a saving of 5,940 miles; from St. Petersburg to Bombay is, by the cape, 11,610 miles, by the canal 6,770 miles — a saving of 4,840 miles; and from New York to Bombay, *via* the cape, 11,520 miles, by the canal 7,920 miles — a saving of 3,600 miles."

The earnings of the company are made by tariff charges upon the vessels, merchandise, and passengers going through the canal. These charges were regulated ten years ago by an international commission of twelve maritime powers, and the scale adopted by it was put in operation. The charges as established are fixed at ten francs per ton, ten per passenger, with other dues for pilotage, anchorage and minor services. The actual cost of the canal is stated at $87,590,000 in round numbers. The net profits for the year 1883, the last reported, amounted to $7,170,000 in round numbers, and the dividend paid to the shareholders in that year amounted to 17.33 per cent. Inasmuch as the total number of shares is about 400,000, England, as the purchaser of 176,602, may be said to own more than two-fifths of the canal.

It is provided by the rules of the company that, aside from the 5 per cent. interest on the shares, the net earnings shall be divided as follows: 15 per cent. to the Egyptian treasury; 10 to the founders' shares; 2 to form invalid fund; 71 as dividend on the 400,000 shares; and 2 to the managing directors. The cost of the canal to the Egyptian government was very heavy, and had much to do with bringing the financial affairs of Egypt into the perplexity which provoked foreign interference. The total cost is given by Mr. McCoan, up to 1875, at about $87,000,000. "Nor is this even," he says, "the full measure of its heavy cost to the country. It has diverted from the native harbors and railroads a large and profitable transit traffic, from which for years to come the treasury will derive little beyond some trifling customs dues. Yet the political gains from it have been great. Its importance to the trade of the world has given Egypt a definite place in the European concert."

The extent to which the maritime use of the canal has grown may be judged by these figures. In 1873, 1,171 vessels, with an aggregate tonnage of 2,085,270, passed through, and the receipts amounted to about $500,000. In 1883, 3,307 vessels, with an aggregate tonnage of 8,106,601 passed through, yielding receipts to the sum of $13,000,000. Of the different maritime nations England sends three-quarters of the vessels and tonnage which go through the canal. In 1883, of the 3,307 vessels, 2,537 were English, 272 were French, 124 were Dutch, 123 were German, 67 were Austrian, 63 were Italian, 51 were Spanish, 18 were Russian, 18 were Norwegian, 12 were Belgian, 9 were Turkish, and 3 were Egyptian.

Some idea is thus gained of the value of the Suez canal to the commercial world dealing with the East. Its political importance should not be ignored. In the event of war, especially of war between Russia and England, the Suez canal would be of special, and almost vital, necessity to England. It would be sorely needed for the transit of her war-ships, troops and war-supplies. England's interest in the canal is, indeed, three-fold. She has a stake in its prosperity as the holder of more than a third of its shares; as the largest commercial State trading with the East; and as the ruler of India, to which the canal offers the nearest route. It is, indeed, the Suez canal which affords England one of her most imperative reasons for keeping her hold on Egypt, through whose territory the canal passes, and to whose administration and military control the canal is subject.

III.

THE GOVERNMENT, PEOPLE AND RESOURCES OF EGYPT.

IN considering the government of Egypt as it now exists it must always be borne in mind that English influence is in reality paramount in Cairo. The Khedive is an absolute ruler. All the laws are promulgated by him, and his will is law throughout the administration. But circumstances have placed the Khedive completely under English influence. The English diplomatic agent, resident at Cairo, guides the Khedive's policy with the force of command. Thus the organization of the Egyptian army and policy, the execution of reforms in Egypt's internal affairs, as well as the regulation of Egyptian finance, are really in the hands of the foreign power which stands before Europe and the world solely accountable for the well-being and solvency of the Egyptian realm.

There is a certain degree of executive and legislative system in the Egyptian administration. The Khedive has his cabinet of five ministers, who preside respectively over foreign affairs, finances, war, interior, public worship and education. The minister of foreign affairs is usually the Prime Minister, who, with the Khedive's assent, selects and appoints his colleagues. Connected in a certain way with the ministry is an English "financial adviser," who has a "consultation voice" in the ministerial council. By a constitutional project put into operation under English influence in 1883, two bodies of a *quasi* legislative character were established. One of these is a legislative council of thirty members, of whom sixteen are chosen by indirect and very restricted suffrage for six years, and fourteen are appointed by the Khedive. The functions of this body are defined to be "to consider petitions addressed to the Khedive, and to give their views on the budget and other matters;" these views being accepted or rejected on the advice of the ministers.

The other public body is called the General Assembly. It comprises the ministers, the members of the legislative council, and forty-six additional members chosen by indirect suffrage for six years. This assembly is empowered to "vote new taxes, give its opinion on every new loan, public works, land-taxes, and on other matters which are submitted to it by the Khedive." The legislative council meets several times each year; the General Assembly at least as often as once in two years. No one can be elected to the latter body who is not able to read and write, or who pays a land tax of less than $250. The electoral body of Egypt, the total population of which is nearly 7,000,000, is less than 1,000,000.

A large reform was also effected in 1883, in the local government of the Egyptian provinces. Over the eight principal towns are placed officials of the rank of Governor. Egypt is also divided into fourteen prefectures, or provinces, governed by *mudirs*. These prefectures are divided into departments, or *kisms*, which are governed by *mamours;* and the departments are again divided into communes, or cantons, governed by *nazirs* and *sheiks*. Each province has its elective legislative council, chosen indirectly by universal suffrage; and there is also a local council for each commune or canton. The village sheik is the tax assessor and gatherer, and is a magistrate and constable in one. The old cruel system of wringing oppressive taxes from the fellahs by the application of the *courbash* — a whip made of hippopotamus hide — is fast going out of existence, owing to the more enlightened methods of tax levying and collecting introduced under English influence.

Other important changes which have been effected in Egyptian affairs within two or three years have been the reorganization of the judicial system, of the police, and of the army. The courts have been to some extent reformed by the continuation of mixed tribunals of Europeans and natives, and the curtailment and regulation of the judicial powers of the *mudirs*. A new criminal code was established in 1884, and a Procureur-General (attorney-general) created to supervise the magisterial system. It may be broadly said that justice is done in Egypt as never before, though there is still much to do before its reign can become supreme. The police system has been consolidated and centralized, and placed under the control of a Director-General at Cairo. The police were formerly under the control of the *mudirs*. In the autumn of 1882 the entire Egyptian army was disbanded, and organized on a new basis. The new army comprised about 6,000 men, and was put under the command of an English general, Sir Evelyn Wood.

From the time of the defeat of Arabi Pasha at Tel-el-Kebir to the present, an English army of occupation has remained in Egypt, garrisoned mainly at Alexandria and Cairo. Thus England holds military as well as political control over the country. This army according to the last reports comprised about 11,000 men, in command of General Stephenson. This of course is exclusive of the forces sent more recently to the Soudan, under the commands respectively of Generals Wolseley and Graham. The principal results of the virtual English protectorate have been, that the *courbash* has been for the most part abolished; the system of public works has been improved; the new tribunals have been put into working order, and the prison system has been materially reformed.

The subjects of the Khedive dwelling in Egypt proper are very diverse in race and traits. They comprise settled Arabs (the large proportion of whom are fellaheen, or peasants, tilling the land), Bedoween (or nomadic Arabs), Turks, Copts, Abyssinians, Nubians, Jews, rayah Greeks, Syrians, Armenians, and Europeans of many nationalities. Of these the settled Arabs form the overwhelming majority, comprising probably four-fifths of the population. It is said that most of these settled Arabs are descendants of the Christian Copts, who apostasized to Islam when the Arabs conquered Egypt in the seventh century. The Arab fellaheens, especially those of lower Egypt, are described as powerful, sturdy men, of a good average height, and notable often for their physical beauty. The women too are finely formed, and have in many cases beautiful teeth and expressive features. McCoan says of the fellaheen that they are "the most patient, the most pacific, the most home-loving, and withal the merriest race in the world." They are temperate, honest and easily content.

As for the wandering Bedoween who swarm in the valleys and deserts of the upper Nile, they present the characteristics which mark nomadic races the world over. It is thought that the Bedoween number in all not far from 300,000, the most important tribes being the Ababdehs and the Bishareen, on the borders and northern regions of the Soudan. The Bedoween are proud, independent, warlike, impulsive and fickle. They present a singular contrast to their settled Arab brethren. They are adventurous and wandering by nature and inheritance. For a few months they settle down on the borders where fertility joins the desert; the rest of the year finds them crossing the dreary wastes, encamping by lovely springs, and flitting with their caravans from oasis to oasis.

Second in the Egyptian population in point of numbers are the Copts, the ancient Christians of the Nile-land. The Copts are regarded as the descendants of the Egyptians of the Rameses and the Pharaohs, though with some admixture of Greek and Persian blood. Most of all the Khedive's subjects the Copts resemble the sculptured faces on the pyramids and obelisks. They are small of stature, full of feature, with straight noses, large lips and large black eyes. They belong to the Jacobite set of Christians, and regard St. Mark as the founder of their faith. But they are probably the most degraded of Christian sects, practising polygamy and circumcision and other Moslem customs. They have, however, good business capacity, and comprise a large proportion of the retail shopkeepers and land agents in Egypt. The Copts may be ranked as the lower middle class of Egyptian society. In upper Egypt many of them are small farmers; and they are employed to some extent in subordinate capacities in the public offices.

The subjugation of Egypt by the Turks resulted naturally in the addition of a Turkish population to the mixed races of the Nile. But nearly all the Turks who followed in the wake of Selim's conquest three and a half centuries ago took up their abode in or near Cairo. They became the dominant official and social caste, and were a sort of aristocracy, who held aloof from their Egyptian fellow-Moslems. After a time, however, the Turks in Egypt lost their social supremacy and their official influence. The offices were taken from them and given to Arabs; and as time went on the Turkish colony decreased in numbers. There are now said to be less than 10,000 Turks in Egypt, mostly settled in the large cities, and engaged in trade or industrial occupations.

Of the remaining races domiciled in Egypt it may be said that the Abyssinians nearly resemble the Copts, alike in religious belief and custom, in physical traits, and in moral and mental characteristics. For the most part they came to Egypt as slaves, and the women are greatly preponderant in number. There are two kinds of Greeks in Egypt: those who claim to be descended from the ancient Greek conquerors, and the modern Greeks who have taken up their abode in the cities, and are the lowest and most worthless of the denizens of the eastern Mediterranean. Lastly, the Jews of Egypt are the most degraded of all oriental Jews. They were long bitterly persecuted, but are much less so in these days of broader toleration. Some of them have risen to high influence as bankers and merchants; but for the most part they are pawnbrokers, usurers, vendors of cheap goods and artisans.

The principal industry of Egypt is and has been for many years the cultivation of the land in what is called the Delta, and along the banks of the Nile. The Delta is an irregular triangle, enclosed between the two branches of the Nile which flow into the

Mediterranean. Its base is about 80 miles in length, and its area about 2,000 square miles. The Delta is fertile, and almost wholly arable. The cultivable land above it, from Cairo as far as Assouan, has an average width, including both banks of the river Nile, of 6 miles; being wider at some points and narrower at others. Of course the limit of this arable land on either side is the line up to which the Nile overflows its banks in the spring. On either side the valley is shut in from the desert regions beyond by ranges of hills and mountains.

There are, moreover, certain valleys which are very fruitful. The chief of these is the valley of Fayoum, 80 miles south-west from Cairo, which, being artificially watered by canals, is luxuriantly fertile over a tract of some 700 square miles. The valley of Fayoum produces in abundance not only rice and grain, but also dates, flax, grapes, cotton, many varieties of fruit, and roses, from which rose-water is made. There are several large oases, too, in Egyptian territory which reward the tiller of the land with profitable crops. The most considerable of these are the Great and Lesser Oases, southward from Fayoum. In all the arable land of Egypt is estimated at not far from 5,000,000 acres, of which 500,000 comprise the landed estates of the Khedive. As has been said, the great mass of farm laborers are the Arab fellaheen.

The most valuable product of Egyptian land is cotton, a plant which was certainly cultivated by the ancient, as it still is by the modern, Egyptians. The revival of cotton-planting took place in 1821 under the auspices of Mehemet Ali. At present it is probable that 1,000,000 acres are yearly sown with this staple. In 1883 cotton to the value of $38,000,000 was exported from Egypt, almost entirely to England. Besides this, cotton-seed was exported to the value of $8,500,000. The next product in value is beans, which are grown in nearly every part of Egypt, and yielded in exports, in

1883, about $5,000,000. Wheat is the third staple, with an export value of $2,725,000.

One of the great industries of Egypt, both in production and in manufacture, is sugar. Egyptian sugar, moreover, competes successfully with the best sugar of France. In 1883 sugar to the value of $2,000,000 was exported from Egypt. Some 80,000 acres are devoted to the cultivation of the sugarcane, of which more than one-half is grown on the Khedive's estates. The late Khedive, Ismail, spent enormous sums in the erection of sugar factories and treacle (molasses) mills. Of the other products of Egypt, ivory was exported in 1883 to the value of $600,000; skins to the value of $625,000; rice $605,000; gum $600,000; maize $200,000; and ostrich feathers $350,000.

The total of Egyptian exports for 1883 was about $61,500,000, of which England received about two-thirds; America received Egyptian products to the amount of $150,000. The imports into Egypt for this same year reached $43,000,000, of which England contributed a little less than one-half. The principal imports consisted of cotton goods, coal, clothing, indigo, timber, wines and spirits, coffee, tobacco, refined sugar and machinery. It may be added that the Egyptian railways now cover lines to the extent of 1,276 miles; that the telegraphs have a total length of about 3,000 miles, and that the number of post-offices in the kingdom is about 172.

IV.

THE SOUDAN.

The country of the Soudan, which has attracted public attention during the past two or three years, is a vast, vague region lying to the south of Egypt proper, and has no well-defined boundaries. The word "Soudan" means "the country of the black men." The Soudan which belongs to Egypt, however, embraces but a small portion of the territory designated by that name; and even of the Soudan of Egypt it is quite impossible to say where, at least on the west and on the south, it begins and ends. Egypt proper may be said to end at the northern borders of the great Nubian desert, its most southerly point on the Nile being the town of Assouan, just below the first cataract. On the east the Egyptian Soudan finds its limit at the Red Sea and Abyssinia.

On the west Egyptian rule has extended itself as far as the important district of Darfour, and includes the province of Kordofan. It is in the south, far up the two branches of the Nile, that the boundaries of the Soudan become the most indefinite. It is certain that General Gordon, during his first administration as governor of the Soudan in 1874-5, carried his conquests up almost to Lake Albert Nyanza, the source itself of the Nile. But the southern limit of the country over which Egypt has actually established authority has been placed, by a recent writer, at Gondokoro. The whole region of the Soudan under Egyptian rule is roughly estimated at 2,500,000 square miles, with a population somewhere between 10,000,000 and 15,000,000. Of this population it is probable that one-third are nomadic Arabs, and the other two-thirds negroes. A majority of the inhabitants, however, both Arab and negro, are believed to be Mahommedans.

The conquest of the northern portion of the Soudan was effected by Mehemet Ali, whose son Ibrahim carried the Egyptian arms to the junction of the White and Blue Niles. At that junction Mehemet founded the fortress town of Khartoum, which afterward became, and still continues to be, the most important emporium and *entrepôt* of the country. It commanded the slave reserves to the south and west, received the supplies of ivory and other products of the desert regions, and gave a formidable point of defence and departure to the military projects of Egypt. For many years after Mehemet's death no effort was made by the Egyptian rulers to extend their dominions in the Soudan. Ismail Pasha, however, formed a vast scheme of aggrandizement, in which he was encouraged by the English in the hope that thereby the hideous slave-trade of the upper Nile might be restricted, if not altogether crushed out.

Ismail made the conquest of Darfour in 1875, and thereby added a large and for the most part fruitful province to his kingdom. Darfour produces wheat, rice, maize and tobacco in abundance, and some cotton. It has mines of copper and iron, and is a prosperous cattle-raising country. It has a thriving trade with Egypt and Arabia in ivory, ostrich feathers, hides, and, it is unpleasant to add, in slaves. Already the fertile and densely populated Shillook country had come under Egyptian control; while the expeditions of Sir Samuel Baker and, soon after, of "Chinese Gordon," undertaken with a primary view of suppressing the slave-trade, served to extend Egyptian rule far up the Nile, and to open communication with regions which had before been, to civilization, as dark as any part of the "Dark Continent." Indeed, so vigorous were Gordon's efforts to this end that he actually established a line of communication from Cairo to the equator, a distance of nearly 3,000 miles.

But the control of the Egyptian Khedives over the Soudan was never complete. It could only be maintained in the settled towns and at the isolated garrison posts. It could not reach out over the deserts, and reduce the vast, wandering, barbarous, swarming Arabs and negroes to submission. Neither Baker nor Gordon could suppress, or more than temporarily limit, the slave-trade. That trade

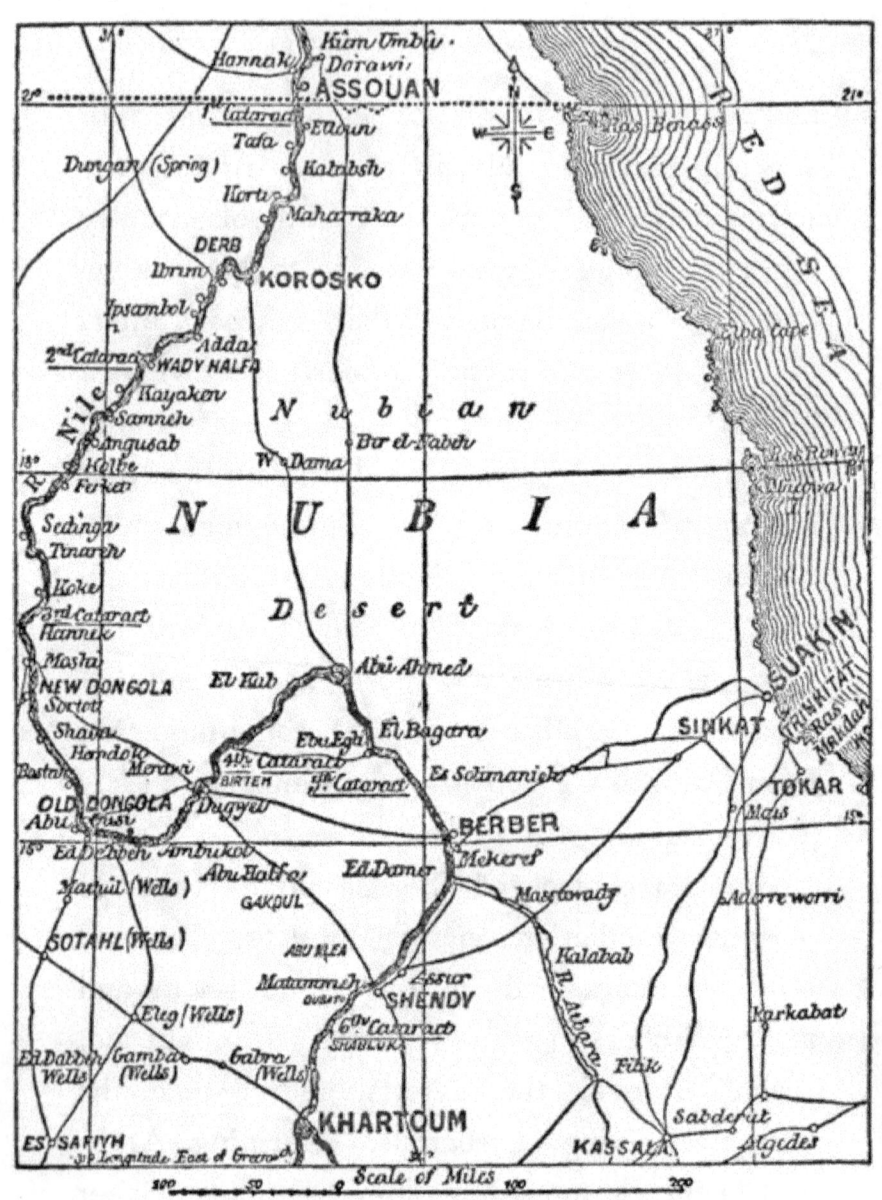

FORTRESS OF THE SOUDAN.

was and is truly " ingrained in every fibre of what may be called social life throughout all Central and Eastern Africa, and no power on earth can extinguish it except by the slow agency of civilization." The channels by which slaves are brought to the Red Sea and shipped to Arabia and other parts of Western Asia, run from the Galla country, the regions of the great southern lakes, and Kordofan; and it has been found impossible to close more than one or two of these channels at a time.

The principal fortress towns of the Soudan which have been garrisoned by Egyptian troops, and from which Egyptian governors have tried to impose the decrees of Cairo, are Khartoum, Dongola, Berber, Shendy, Sennaar, all of which are on the upper Nile, and all except Sennaar, below the junction of the two branches; Kassala, which stands not far from the Abyssinian frontier, near the Akbara — the largest affluent of the Nile which empties into it below Khartoum; and Suakin, a seaport on the Red Sea, which is 240 miles from Berber, the nearest point to Suakin on the Nile. An abortive attempt was made by Ismail to construct a railway up the valley of the Nile from Cairo to Khartoum; but this railway up to the present time has only been completed about 200 miles to Siout; the distance from Cairo to Khartoum being about 1,200 miles.

The rule of the Egyptians in the Soudan has been from first to last oppressive and capriciously cruel. Taxes have been imposed with rigor, and have been collected with ruthless severity. The Khedives have enforced conscriptions, by which the Arabs and negroes have been compelled to enter the Egyptian army, and to fight, if need there were, their own tribes and countrymen. It is said that at times no less than 30,000 Soudanese have been enrolled among the Egyptian forces. The people of the Soudan are composed of fierce, warlike races, as they have abundantly shown in the recent campaigns, and they have always resented the rule of their northern conquerors. They could only be kept from open revolt by the stringent application of military methods. The slave-traders resented interference with their inhuman but profitable commerce; while that part of the population which eagerly desired the suppression of the slave-trade looked with despair on the futile attempts of the Egyptian pashas, aided by English governors, to put it down.

It only needs a brief glimpse of the Soudan — of the character of its inhabitants; its vast regions of desert, interspersed with fertile provinces, oases and rich valleys; the conditions of its means of subsistence; the oppressive methods of Egyptian rule; the opportunities afforded by the demoralization of Egyptian affairs; the appeal made by a pretended prophet, at a ripe moment, to the fanaticism and superstition of barbarous Moslems — to explain the formidable revolt which has destroyed garrisons, sacrificed Gordon, and long defied the prowess of English arms. The events which have led to these results properly belong to another chapter.

V.

EL MAHDI, THE "FALSE PROPHET."

HAVING briefly described the building up of the modern kingdom of Egypt; the construction of the Suez canal, and its bearing upon European politics and especially upon English interests; the present status of the Egyptian government, and the political control of England therein; and the region of the Soudan, upon which public interest was recently intent; I resume the narration of the events which have followed the overthrow of Arabi Pasha by the English and the consequent strengthening of the English hold on Egypt.

Arabi's defeat and capture left Egypt, indeed, completely at the mercy of England. With him the flower of the Egyptian army had been overthrown and dispersed; and it had become necessary that the Khedive's dominions should be

ENGLAND IN EGYPT. 63

protected by English troops. While, therefore, the English cabinet reiterated the declaration that they intended to evacuate Egypt, and to leave the Khedive entirely to himself, just as soon as the country could be restored to order and settled government, as a fact English influence was now supreme at Cairo, and increased English garrisons were established at Cairo and Alexandria. But scarcely had Arabi been safely consigned to captivity in Ceylon when a fresh revolt broke out against Egyptian rule in the distant and difficult region of the Soudan, which was destined to prove far more obstinate than that of the ex-Minister of War. This revolt was headed by a personage so remarkable, with a career so dramatic, that some account of him will not be out of place.

About four years ago a startling rumor crept through the Mohammedan populations of Africa and Arabia that a man claiming to be the later Messiah of Islam, the successor of Mohammed, the chief of a new crusade, had made his appearance south of the Nubian desert. What gave greater importance to the rumor was, that for generations there has floated in the East a saying that in the latter part of this century a new prophet would arise; would gather to him the scattered forces of the faithful; and would restore the Moslem faith and power to their ancient height. The appearance of the new self-styled "Mahdi" was at first discredited. At Constantinople and at Mecca the news was received with indifference and contempt. Many an impostor has thus attempted to foist himself with prophetic authority on Islam, only to be overwhelmed with disaster and to be driven into obscurity and disgrace. But the stories of the latest Mahdi kept coming from the barbarous regions of the upper Soudan. It was said that a large though savage army had flocked to his standard; that the tribes on the banks of the Blue and the White Nile were giving in their allegiance to him; and that the disaffection which he had stirred up was spreading even among the warlike Bedoween between the Nile and the Red Sea.

The undoubted existence and the increasing strength of the Mahdi could at last no longer be ignored at the centres of Mohammedan authority. A serious alarm seized the court of the Sultan-Caliph, and grave councils were held in the great temple at Mecca. Then the Grand Cherif of Mecca, the highest of the high-priests of Islam, issued his proclamation declaring the new claimant to be an impostor, and warning the faithful to avoid his standard and to resist his pretensions. It was supposed that this decree would at once act on the superstitious minds of the African Mohammedans, and that the self-claimed Mahdi would be deserted and, like previous impostors, disappear. But this result did not follow. The Cherif's fulmination did not serve in the least to check the growth of the Mahdi's cause. Gradually his following increased; and now, assuming the militant *rôle* of Mohammed, he began an aggressive campaign. He set to himself the task first of wresting the Soudan from the rule of Egypt; and did not hesitate to proclaim that he intended to pursue the conquest of all the African Mohammedan States.

The Mahdi's career seems to have been attended from the first with almost unvarying good fortune. More than one Egyptian stronghold fell into the hands of his rabble and fanatic horde. At last the Egyptian Khedive, miserable as his situation was, had no alternative but to attempt the suppression of this fresh revolt against his authority. The defeat of Arabi Pasha at Tel-el-Kebir had deprived the Khedive of his best troops, and he was forced to send an inferior armament against the rebellious prophet. A force of 10,000 Egyptians and Nubians, under command of Hicks Pasha, an Englishman, marched against the Mahdi, who was already threatening the fortresses of the upper Nile. The hostile armies met at El Obeid, west of the White Nile. The encounter was short and savage. Its appalling result was, that Hicks Pasha and his force were not only overwhelmingly defeated, but were almost to a man destroyed on the field of battle by the enraged legions of the prophet.

All Europe and the East shuddered at this frightful disaster, which was a terrific blow at the rule of the Khedive. It also shook the

Sultan's throne, and carried dismay to the holy places of Mecca. The prestige of the Mahdi was immensely increased by his success. It fell with telling effect upon the ears and imagination of the Mohammedan races. Victory seemed to give sanction to the Mahdi's claim. It was said that his army at El Obeid numbered at least 200,000 men, comprised of dervishes, Bedoween, mulattoes, and some regular troops supplied with fire-arms. Of course his followers rapidly increased after the overthrow of Hicks Pasha's army; and now the Mahdi seriously threatened Khartoum and the Egyptian fortresses protecting the Soudan at Dongola, Berber, Sennaar and other places between the upper Nile and the Red Sea.

The Mahdi's name was Mohammed Achmet. He was a native of the province of Dongola, a fortified town on the Nile between the third and fourth cataracts, and bordering upon the great Nubian desert. He was said to be of pure Arab blood; and this was fortunate for him, since none but an Arab could ever hope to impose a prophetic authority upon Islam. His grandfather was a Moslem priest. His father, Abdullah, was a carpenter. Early in the Mahdi's boyhood the family moved to Shendy, not far from Berber. Here the young Achmet was apprenticed to his uncle, a boatman. This uncle having one day beaten him, the boy ran away to Khartoum, where he entered a free school kept by a fakir (learned man, head of a sect of dervishes). Achmet studied hard, and especially absorbed himself in learning the doctrines of Mohammedanism as taught by the sheik of the shrine of Hoggiali. He then removed to a similar school near Berber, attached to another shrine much reverenced by the natives. After passing some time at this and other schools Achmet was himself ordained as a sheik, at a village called Aradup, in the year 1870, and he at once took up his abode in this sacred capacity on the Island of Abba, in the White Nile.

It was at Abba that Achmet entered upon those practices and began no doubt to prepare himself for that mission which have since attracted to him the allegiance of such formidable numbers of Mohammedans. He dug a deep cave on the island, and made it a habit to retire for prayer and contemplation into its darkest recesses. There he would repeat for hours together one of the names of the Deity, which exercise was accompanied by fasting, the burning of incense and attitudes of abject humility. His renown as a man of saintly character spread far and wide. He grew rich on the offerings of the pious, and married several wives, being always careful to choose them from influential and wealthy Arab families.

At last, in 1881, he openly announced himself to be the Mahdi foretold by Mohammed, whose advent had been predicted for that very year. He sent messages to the sheiks and fakirs round about, declaring that he had a divine mission to reform Islam; to establish a universal equality, a universal law, a universal religion, and a community of goods; and to destroy all — whether Mohammedan or Christian — who refused to believe him and to accept him as a true prophet. Just as, in Christianity, Christ superseded the Mosaic dispensation, so the Mahdi claims to have been sent by Allah to renew the old covenant of God with man. By these bold assertions the Mahdi soon secured a hearing, then a following. Many of the sheiks who had long observed his austere piety were easily persuaded to believe him inspired, and adopted his cause with Oriental ardor and enthusiasm. He soon found himself accepted, not only by large numbers of the population in the regions of the Blue and the White Nile, but even among the wandering tribes of the Nubian and Soudan deserts.

The Mahdi was fortunate in being able to work upon the imagination of the races whom he sought to win, by certain circumstances and coincidences which seemed to give him a resemblance to the Prophet Mohammed. These the ignorant and credulous Arabs were not slow to magnify into striking proofs of the Mahdi's divine mission. When they heard that he bore upon his face certain peculiar marks symbolical of a true prophetic character; that there was a difference in the length of his arms and also in the color of his eyes, — defects which appertained to the great Mohammed himself; that not only was his name, but that of his parents, Mohammed, their enthusiasm was aroused and their faith became fixed. He could assert that, like the great prophet, he had been forced to fly for his life when he put forth his startling claim; and that, again like the founder of Islam, he had been able in spite of repeated obstacles to explain the causes of his ill-fortune, and to keep his followers with him in adversity as well as in victory.

These things he said he had accomplished by timely revelations from Allah. Thus it was that he carried his cause through the Soudan, and made himself reverenced as one who was in constant communion with Heaven, and who had acquired the exalted power of working miracles. The Mahdi's example was followed by other fakirs in the Soudan, who rose to rival his pretensions and to claim the divine office of prophet for themselves. No sooner, however, did such rivalry rear its head than the Mahdi assailed his foe, and with all the savage and pitiless ferocity of Mohammed himself overcame him and crushed him and his followers to the earth.

Those who have seen this remarkable man

describe him as tall, slim, straight, with the true Arab creamy complexion, black hair cut close to the skull, and a black beard descending to a point after the Arab fashion. His eyes were dark and piercing, one eye being black and the other brown. His manner was stern, serious, and often absent and distraught, as if in deep contemplation. He was very reticent, giving his orders in few words, and was active and alert in all his proceedings. The Mahdi proved himself a man of extraordinary ability. He was a warrior of the fierce, impetuous, obstinate Arab type. He kindled to fiery ardor on the battle-field. He was yet cautious and adroit as a strategist. His career showed him to be cunning and far-seeing. He seems to have maintained a wonderful efficiency of military organization among the barbarians who so eagerly followed his standard, and to have had the ability to create an army out of the most unpromising materials. In the midst of warlike conflict he maintained his religious pretensions and practices. He spent much time in solitude, prayer, fasting and silent contemplation. He professed to seek daily the counsels and commands of Allah. He claimed to communicate with the spirit of Mohammed, and to receive from the great prophet the inspiration of his warlike movements.

Of imposing personal appearance, he sustained the faith and loyalty of his followers wherever he himself was present and in their sight. He made no secret of his design to reconquer Islam, to sweep the Christians from Egypt, Turkey, Tunis, Algiers, and even from India and Turkistan. He aimed to refound Islam and to reform it. His methods, like those of the great prophet, were not only militant but relentless. Massacre and desolation marked the places across which the tornado of his barbaric hordes had swept. By fire and sword the old foundations of Islam were to be renewed. His exploits made him, for the time at least, well-nigh the absolute master of the Soudan. The sudden and mysterious death of the Mahdi, a few months after his many triumphs had culminated in the capture of Khartoum and the immolation of Gordon, abruptly cut short a career the conquests and conversions of which could not have easily been forecast.

VI.

ENGLAND IN EGYPT AND THE SOUDAN.

WHILE the revolt of the Mahdi wore from the beginning a religious aspect, while his first claim to attention and support was derived from his assumption of prophecy, the movement of which he took the lead soon became political in its objects. It was the long misrule of Egypt in the Soudan, a misrule marked by cruelty, robbery and oppression, which rallied to him his rude armies of Arab and negro barbarians. The dominion of Egypt had become simply intolerable. The rebellion of Arabi Pasha, though unsuccessful, aroused a kindred spirit of resistance among the warlike tribes of the deserts and the upper Nile; and the Mahdi, with his prophetic pretensions, came in the nick of time to lend superstitious zeal and military ability to the movement.

Of the numbers who flocked to the Mahdi's standard, and who afterwards followed him in his remarkable career, no estimate can be made. It is certain that his forces varied greatly with the changing phases of the war. One tribe deserted him, while another promptly filled the gap after having opposed his progress. A decisive success probably always had the effect of swelling his ranks. It is very likely that the conjecture of a recent writer that in all the Mahdi's forces there had been 200,000 warriors at one time is approximately accurate. The Mahdi succeeded in capturing several of the Egyptian garrisons before the English came to oppose his further advance; and, as fast as a garrison was taken, it was massacred by the Mahdi's ruthless followers.

The first step taken by England when it had become apparent that the revolt of the Soudan was assuming dangerous proportions was to advise the Khedive, in a tone which was virtually a command, to abandon the Soudan altogether, to withdraw his garrisons if possible, and leave the destinies of the country to its own people. To this the Khedive assented. But it soon became apparent that the Egyptian government was too weak to attempt the withdrawal of the garrisons, and England was forced, very much against her will, to follow up the advice given to the Khedive by undertaking the relief of the garrisons herself.

This decision was hastened by an event which took place near Suakin. An Egyptian force under Valentine Baker was overwhelmingly defeated in its attempt to relieve the garrison of Sinkat, a few miles inland, by Osman Digna, one of the Mahdi's Generals. Osman Digna, who afterwards played a notable part in the war, was said to be a Frenchman by birth, to have been educated in the military schools at Cairo, and to have become a Mussulman in early youth. After the defeat of Baker, Osman Digna threatened Suakin itself with an Arab force estimated at not less than 30,000 men. An English expedition, together with a naval force, was at once despatched to the Red Sea. But before it could act effectively the Egyptian garrisons at Sinkat and Tokar had yielded to the enemy, and had been for the most part massacred.

The English under General Graham now entered upon a vigorous campaign against Osman Digna. It was recognized that in his destruction only lay the safety of Suakin, if not that of all the garrisons in the northern Soudan. Osman's Arabs swarmed in the hills westward of Suakin; and the English advanced to confront him on the Suakin-Berber road. Graham inflicted two crushing defeats on the rebel chief at Teb and Tamai, and it seemed for a while as if Osman's military power was completely broken. Public opinion in England urged at this juncture that a part, at least, of Graham's force should continue its march across the desert to Berber, and thus relieve not only Berber, but Khartoum. But, to the general astonishment, Graham with his troops withdrew by order of the English cabinet, and after two fruitless victories the campaign near the Red Sea came to an end.

The problem which now presented itself was how to relieve Khartoum, still held by a faithful Egyptian garrison, and the most important military position in the Soudan. The relief of Khartoum was a much more formidable task than the defeat of Osman; since Khartoum was far away amid the interior deserts, and could only be reached by any route with infinite difficulty and danger. The councils of the English cabinet were greatly perplexed how to accomplish it. The fear of becoming deeply involved in a distant and expensive war with Arab fanatics vied with the responsibilities which England had assumed in Egypt, and the necessity of protecting Egypt from an invasion by the False Prophet. England had virtually pledged herself to rescue the garrisons in the Soudan, and could not with honor retreat from her engagement.

A strange, striking, but as the result proved futile policy was adopted by Mr. Gladstone and his colleagues. Yet this policy had this merit, that if it succeeded it would have cost little in men or money. General Charles Gordon had long been famous for his military genius, his adventurous and fearless spirit, his wonderful skill in dealing with barbarous races, and his high capacity for administration in Mohammedan communities. He had fought with gallantry and brilliant success in the Chinese rebellion. He had done excellent service as Governor of the Soudan, where he had apparently won the respect and allegiance of the nomad tribes. He had waged a vigorous warfare against the slave-trade. He was full of ardor, daring, and self-confidence. The English cabinet resolved to send General Gordon to the Soudan, unattended by any military force, but empowered to procure the withdrawal of the Egyptian garrisons and to establish a settled government by any means which he might find it best to adopt.

Gordon set out for Khartoum in February, 1884. He went almost alone, his companions being two or three officers and an Arab convoy. His only weapon was an ordinary walking-stick. He went up the Nile from Cairo to Korosko, and thence struck across the Nubian desert, in constant peril of his life, surrounded by hostile or suspicious tribes, and exposed to the many dangers of the desert. But he passed it safely, rejoined the Nile at Abu

Hamed, and thence proceeded up the river to Khartoum.

At the Soudanese capital he was received with a welcome which seemed to give bright promise of the success of his mission. With his unresting zeal he at once began the task committed to him. He found the garrison stanch and many of the surrounding tribes not unfriendly. He strengthened the fortifications of Khartoum and other places in the vicinity, established order so far as his authority extended, and was even able to send down the river to Berber a number of the Egyptians and Europeans who had been living in Khartoum. At first all seemed to go well with Gordon and his purposes, and his reports were cheerful and sanguine. But as the spring and then the summer came on, untoward events took place, and the prospect of his success became constantly more doubtful. Berber fell into the hands of the Mahdi's adherents, and so Khartoum was cut off from communication with Cairo by the Nubian desert; and gradually but steadily the swarming legions of the Mahdi closed around Khartoum itself.

Gordon appealed to England for help, and when help did not come he loudly denounced the English cabinet for their dilatoriness and vacillation. Ere long the fact became clear that not only was Gordon unable to withdraw the Khartoum or any other garrison, but that he himself could not get away from the beleaguered town at the junction of the two Niles. A long period of hesitation and unsettled policy on the part of the Gladstone cabinet ensued. A desperate hope was clung to that something might yet happen to avoid the necessity of sending out a rescuing force. The cabinet drifted among daily changing counsels. Meanwhile Gordon's situation became constantly more precarious, and at last the pressure of overwhelming public opinion, and the obligation of national honor, compelled the cabinet to take decisive action.

Late in the autumn of 1884 a British army under General Lord Wolseley (who had won his peerage at Tel-el-Kebir), was despatched to the Soudan for the avowed purpose of rescuing Gordon and relieving Khartoum. Two routes were open by which the army might reach the scene of action: one by way of the Red Sea to Suakin, and thence by the desert route of 240 miles to Berber on the Nile, and by the Nile to Khartoum; the other directly up the Nile to the great bend or loop made by the river at Dongola, thence by the Bayuda desert across to Shendy, and so by river to the Soudanese capital. The latter route was at last chosen; and after a difficult and wearisome passage up the Nile Lord Wolseley with his troops established headquarters at Korti, a short distance south of Dongola.

The plan of Lord Wolseley's campaign was quickly developed. While remaining himself at Korti he decided to send two forces on separate lines of advance. Not only Khartoum, but Berber, was in the hands of the Mahdi's adherents, and it seemed necessary that Berber as well as Khartoum should be rescued by the English. Accordingly General Earle was despatched with a force of about 2,500 men up the great bend of the Nile, with a view of attacking and reducing Berber; while General Stewart, with a force of about the same numerical strength, took up his march eastward across the Bayuda desert, with the intent to strike the Nile opposite Shendy. The distance traversed by Stewart over this desert is about 200 miles.

The main interest of the campaign centred upon Stewart's expedition. It was more perilous and difficult than that of Earle up the river, and it aimed more directly at the principal object of the English in the Soudan, — the rescue of Gordon. The march across the desert was conducted with masterly skill. Twice Stewart and his well-disciplined troops were assailed by great numbers of Arabs, first at Abu Klea wells, and then a few miles further east, and on both occasions the enemy were thoroughly routed. After a march of a little over a week Stewart's force came in sight of the Nile and established their camp at Gubat, on its left bank, a short distance south of Metemmeh. The camp was well fortified, and successive convoys soon supplied it with an abundance of supplies and ammunition.

The next step was to communicate if practicable with Gordon at Khartoum. The river above Gubat, though difficult, seemed at least possible for navigation. It was determined to despatch two steamers, which had been sent down the river some time before by Gordon, to the Soudan capital, under the command of Sir Charles Wilson. Sir Charles accordingly set forth on his adventurous voyage on January 24, 1885. As the steamers passed up the Nile they were assailed by the Arabs who lined the banks, and who maintained a heavy fire on the steamers, in some places using Krupp guns. On January 28 Sir Charles found himself opposite the island of Tuti, just north of Khartoum. No sooner had his steamers made their appearance, however, than a hot fire opened upon them, both from Tuti and from Omdurman and Khartoum. It then became startlingly apparent that Khartoum had fallen into the hands of the Mahdi.

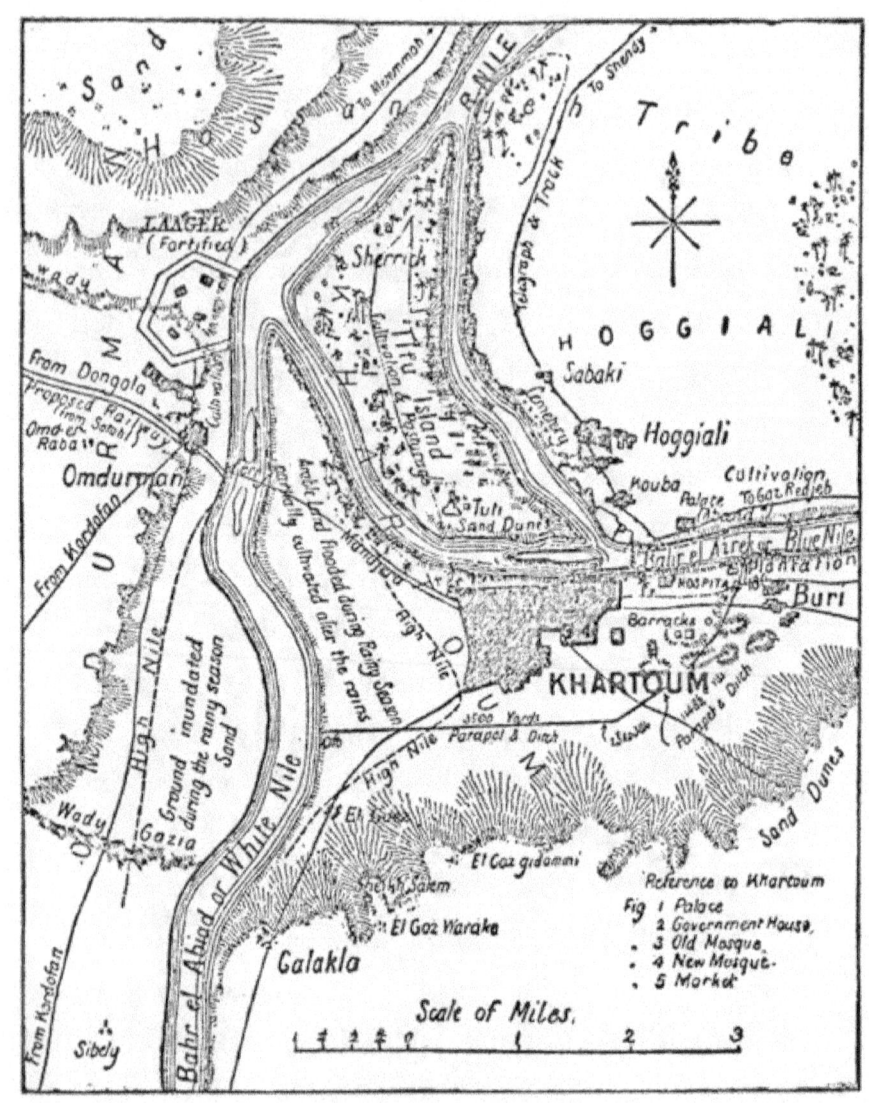

KHARTOUM AND ENVIRONS.

Sir Charles boldly pushed up stream, in the midst of a deadly rifle-fire, to within a mile of the city itself. He saw the Mahdi's flag floating from its ramparts, and swarms of the Mahdi's followers going about in its streets. He then ordered his steamers to retreat down the river, which they did under a shower of bullets. When they reached the sixth cataract one of the steamers was hopelessly wrecked among the rocks, and its men and stores were with difficulty transferred to the other steamer. Soon after, the other steamer was also wrecked below the Shabluka cataract, and Sir Charles was forced to land with his party on a sandy island, whence he sent row-boats to Gubat with the intelligence of the fall of Khartoum and of his own perilous plight. Boats were at once despatched to his rescue, and the expedition soon reached the English camp in safety.

Khartoum had fallen on January 26, two days before the arrival of Sir Charles Wilson's steamers. It appeared that certain Arabs within the city — the chief of whom was one

Farag Pasha — had betrayed the garrison, and while warning the soldiers to keep watch on the defences at one end of the city had opened the gates to the Mahdi and his adherents at the other end. Gen. Gordon himself had been killed in the street in the *melée* which followed, and a large part of the garrison had been cruelly massacred. The Mahdi had long held Omdurman, a fortified place on the banks of the White Nile, opposite Khartoum; and it was from this place that he had crossed the river, and had availed himself of the treachery of Farag and his confederates.

The Stewart expedition had thus been too late to effect the rescue for which an English army had come to the Soudan. General Stewart himself, moreover, had been wounded at Abu Klea, and soon after the return of Wilson, died. Earle's expedition up the great bend of the Nile was still pressing forward towards Abu Hamed. But in a great battle with the Arabs, which took place soon after, General Earle was also killed. Lord Wolseley had now lost his two principal lieutenants; and although the troops in both expeditions had fought with heroic gallantry, and had endured extraordinary hardship with unfaltering patience, it now became evident that to pursue an active campaign in either direction would be futile. The next phase of the war, therefore, was the retreat of both expeditions across the desert and down the river, until once more Wolseley's entire force had gathered in his camp at Korti. Wolseley then transferred his headquarters to Dongola for the summer, and the Nile campaign came to an end.

The scene of the war was now shifted to Suakin on the Red Sea. The British cabinet resolved that while Wolseley lay through the hot weather on the Nile, in inaction, an attempt should be made to effect the only object which now remained — the reduction of Khartoum and the defeat of the Mahdi — by the Suakin-Berber route. It was decided to build a railway across the desert from the Red Sea to the Nile, with its termini at Suakin and Berber. But Osman Digna, whom Sir Gerald Graham had apparently so effectually crushed the year before, had recovered strength and confidence by the fall of Khartoum, and now infested the neighborhood of Suakin with a formidable force. Once more Graham was despatched with troops — among whom was a contingent of Indian Sikhs — to confront his old foe. A series of battles was fought in the region of Támai, where the victories of a year before had been won. The English victories were not as decisive as they had before been; yet the result of them seems to have been discouraging to the Arab chief.

At this juncture the English government at last came to a decided resolution. It was determined to abandon altogether the attempt to recapture Khartoum, to withdraw the troops from the Nile valley, to stop work on the Suakin-Berber railway, and to leave only a small garrison at Suakin. So all operations in the Soudan came to an end, and the chapter of that part of the English interference in Egypt, which related to the Soudan, was closed. Meanwhile the death of the

Mahdi, and the struggle among rival chiefs for the command which he vacated, brought demoralization to the savage insurgents, and they ceased to threaten Egypt proper with any formidable menace. Osman Digna, the ablest of the Mahdi's generals, appears to have been killed in the late summer of 1885, and thus the Soudanese revolt lost the last of its able and conspicuous chiefs.

The certainty that General Gordon's life had been sacrificed profoundly shocked and saddened not only England but all of the Christian world, which had fixed its attention and its admiration on the hero of Khartoum. This feeling was universal, as well with those who sympathized with the effort of the Soudanese to repel the foreign invader, as with those who wished well to the English arms. The spectacle of the valiant, self-forgetful, solitary soldier, staying for a year by his own might the waves of revolt; ready to ransom the lives of his black people by his own blood; matching his brave soul, in solitude and abandonment, against the daily dangers which beset the garrison and the people he was struggling to save; faithful every moment to his desperate task; and leaving a name, brightest, like the setting sun, at its sinking out of sight—deeply and impressively touched the heart of all mankind.

The most recent feature of the Egyptian situation is an international settlement of Egyptian finances. England, unwilling any longer to be solely responsible for the debts of Egypt, called together a conference of the great powers, which was held in London in the summer of 1884. The powers were not averse from assuming a joint responsibility with England in guaranteeing a new Egyptian loan; but there was a disagreement as to the method of adjusting the Egyptian revenue, and the conference dissolved without taking any action. Then England sent the Earl of Northbrook to Cairo to investigate the financial condition; and on receiving his report reopened negotiations with the powers on the subject.

The final result was, that an agreement was arrived at by England, France, Austria, Germany, Russia and Turkey, in March, 1885, by which a loan of $45,000,000 is to be raised on their joint guarantee; England is to make searching inquiry into the Egyptian revenue; foreigners in Egypt (hitherto exempt) are to be taxed; the sum of $1,575,000 is to be paid in yearly until the loan is completed; and the interest is to be a first charge on the revenues assigned to the debt. The supervision of this loan is left to a committee, or *caisse*, composed of delegates of the several powers. At the same time a sub-commission was appointed to consider and report on an international compact securing the freedom and neutrality of the Suez canal, and establishing rules as to the use of the canal in time of war. At the time of writing, this sub-commission has not concluded its labors.

In spite, however, of this entrance of all the powers into a joint interference in Egyptian finance, and whatever may be the fate of the Soudan, England's political grip on Egypt proper remains as firm, and seems as likely to be indefinitely prolonged, as ever. Above all, in view of a war certain, sooner or later, to take place between England and Russia in the East, it is necessary for England to retain control of the land through which the Suez canal takes its course, even although the use of that water-way becomes subject to international restrictions. Gibraltar is the gateway between the Atlantic and the Mediterranean. Egypt, by reason of the Suez canal, has become the gateway between the Mediterranean and the Asiatic waters. England holds the one, and politically dominates the other. By Gibraltar she secures unresisted access to the historic sea which has for so many centuries formed the water-way by which to approach southern Europe. By the control of Egypt, and so in a certain sense at least of the Suez canal, the Mediterranean has ceased to be for English merchantmen and men-of-war a *cul-de-sac*, and has become an outlet and highway to the rich territories over which England holds sway in the Orient.

In brief, England is in Egypt mainly for the same reason that she has so long resisted the capture of Constantinople by Russia ; that she has jealously watched the encroachments of Russia in Asia Minor and Central Asia ; that she has propped and bolstered up the tottering empire of the Turk ; that she has everywhere, and at a cost of millions of money and thousands of brave soldiers, guarded the approaches from Europe to Asia : England is in Egypt mainly because England is in India. She has long feared that the day would come — and it seems, indeed, to be not far distant — when she must fight a mighty conflict in order to hold against her Tartar and Cossack rival her splendid Indian dependency; and it is probable that, when the conflict comes, the troops of England, overleaping all restrictions, will hasten by the Suez canal to the Orient, there to meet face to face, in the gorges of Afghanistan and perhaps in the valley of the Indus, the invading legions of the White Czar.

www.ingramcontent.com/pod-product-compliance
Lightning Source LLC
Chambersburg PA
CBHW020901160426
43192CB00007B/1029